How to Talk Catholic*

and still get lunch invitations

A COMMUNICATION GUIDE FOR MINISTERING IN THE REAL WORLD

S. James Meyer

twentythirdpublications.com

In deep appreciation for all who have found ways to love God and neighbor without ever using the word "magisterium."

Twenty-Third Publications
One Montauk Avenue, Suite 200
New London, CT 06320
(860) 437-3012 or (800) 321-0411
www.twentythirdpublications.com

Copyright © 2020 S. James Meyer. All rights reserved. No part of this publication may be reproduced in any manner without prior written permission of the publisher. Write to the Permissions Editor.

ISBN: 978-1-62785-514-3
Printed in the U.S.A.

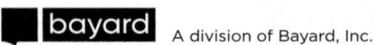

A division of Bayard, Inc.

In the beginning was the WORD

followed by a lot of other words

and all these words
meant something important.

Because that's what words do.
They express and share ideas
that touch hearts and stir souls.

At least they should.

INTRODUCTION

When I first heard the word "apostolic," I was smitten. Its meaning is rich and rooted, and I liked how its roundness rolled from my mouth. Mostly, the word made me feel both smart and holy, a combination I guess I needed at the time.

But when you drop a word like "apostolic" into banter with the neighbors between games of backyard Corn Hole, you get ignored. Do it a second time and you won't be invited back. This is not pushback against religion or Catholicism. The same holds true for words like "ontological" and "syllogistic." Such words are like bread knives; they're keen and have a purpose in the kitchen, but you shouldn't pull them out on the bus.

I wrote this booklet because the Catholic Diocese of Green Bay asked me to. Well, I'm not sure this is what they had in mind, but God bless 'em for letting me and the Spirit hash it out. I'm very grateful for that because I'm sure I make their palms sweat at times.

It's worth pausing for a hat tip to Bishop David Ricken and his Round Table for their vision and courage in this regard. Upon deep-dive introspection, they arrived at a point of illumination: the Catholic Church is great at connecting with people who understand the Catholic Church, but not so hot at connecting with those who do not. And most do not, including many members of the Catholic Church.

Please be forewarned—we're going to have a little fun here, maybe even laugh at ourselves a bit. This doesn't mean church-speak is a trivial thing. I'll be first to advocate for Catholic literacy. Seriously. I once had a confirmation candidate ask me to explain the difference between Pentecost and holocaust. That's kind of a big deal.

Overall, however, if you're going to play in Texas, you gotta have a fiddle in the band, or so the lyrics say. And that means you'd better understand the difference between a fiddle and a violin. The Catholic Church has a habit of playing concertos at barn dances and then complaining that everyone is leaving the party. These pages offer a guide to meeting people where they're at, which is a prerequisite to walking life's journey with them.

Be like God and keep it simple.

So Moses, wandering up a mountain to solve the mystery of the orange glow, comes face to face with God. GOD. Now, I've had to come face to face with some harsh truths, but never THE TRUTH. I've been humbled when facing rejection, dejection, and imperfection. I've been brought to my knees by the superior wisdom of my wife and children. I can't imagine how face-down-in-the-dirt I'd be before God. Good Lord!

Moses, being a mere mortal (keep in mind this is all before he became Holy Moses), is overwhelmed. God is giving him his marching orders and God won't take *no* for an answer. Moses isn't sold on the plan. Stuttering and stumbling for a verbal foothold, he tries one last tactic to show God how ill-conceived this is. "Who will I say sent me?" he asks. It's a fair question. They're going to want to know if Moses is blowing smoke or if he has some muscle backing him up.

God's cheerful, delightful, and almost flippant response is, "I am who I am." That's it. Let's give that space to hang in the air for a moment:

I am who I am.

Perhaps sensing Moses' consternation, God shortens it: "Tell the

Israelites *I am* has sent me to you." (The italics are mine. God never actually emblazoned this text into stone.)

Just like that, the briefest sentence in the history of language, a sentence with only two words and three characters, becomes the most profound statement ever spoken. I am. The Alpha and the Omega. The Creator of all creation. The source of all life and love. I am. It is simultaneously a gross understatement and a profound super statement. It says hardly anything and all of everything. Genius. I am.

Here's the kicker: If God—GOD—can effectively self-identify with such profound simplicity, why can't we talk about following God without using words like "ecclesiastical," "evangelization," and "consubstantial"?

The intention here is not to incite some sort of churchwide vocabulary reform. Let's not get crazy. I might be a sunshine idealist about the Catholic faith, but I'm a rainy-day realist about the Catholic Church. Coadjutor and presbyterate, like mitres, are probably here to stay whether they're good ideas or not. But that doesn't mean we have to trim them with gold piping and parade them around the show ring at the county fair.

The purpose here is to inspire the faithful at ground level, Christ's feet on the street, to speak and write from the mindset of the audience, not from the mindset of the institution. This is, after all, what Jesus did. He spoke of wheat, weeds, wine, sheep, shepherds, and other things with which his audience could relate. He passed up the opportunity to pontificate on repressing the radiance of soul and spoke instead about not keeping your lamp under a bushel.

And that's the whole point—we're much more engaging when we sound relatable and compassionate rather than highbrow and institutional.

LESSON 1

Be like God and keep it simple.

STUFF TO PONDER AND DISCUSS

- How do people encounter God when they're in conversation with you?
- Using only words you would use when out for dinner with friends, how many names for God can you identify?
- What's another way to say "Catholic" using only one- and two-syllable words?

Be authentic and relatable, using words people understand.

As an undergraduate studying creative writing, I thought I should "get" poetry. I fancied myself as some sort of intellectual sophisticate who would casually swirl brandy in a snifter while quoting Walt Whitman. But I lacked the money for brandy and the depth for metaphor. I didn't understand poetry at all.

So I faked it by drinking cheap wine from a dime store goblet and name-dropping poets like baseball fans do with ballplayers. I'm certain it sounded pathetic, like dialog from a bad after school movie in the 1980s.

All I really knew about poetry were the old school mechanics like structure and rhyme patterns, and I'd show off this knowledge by wedging the term "iambic pentameter" into conversations about unrelated things. "The forecast calls for five hot days and cool nights, sort of an iambic pentameter of temperatures." In this way I could at least impress myself, which was fortunate since I obviously spent a lot of time alone.

Fifty cent words can cover a nickel's depth only for so long. Sooner or later the winds of authenticity blow back the curtain and you're left standing there exposed. From that moment on, ouch. "At the end of the day," the poet Maya Angelou famously said, "people won't remember what you said or did, they will remember how you made them feel." Big, smart sounding words that few people understand leave everyone else feeling distant.

Helpful hint for people in the religion business: "distant" is not the emotion you're going for.

As a parallel here, several research studies have shown that healthcare patients don't trust physicians who speak in medical jargon nearly as much as they trust doctors who use ordinary language. There is a sense that while the first might know a lot about disease, the second understands me, the patient. We are far more apt to trust people who relate to us.

Now, apply that same idea to your local parish priest. Who do you think people trust more—Fr. Mike who refers to the parish staff as Lisa, Sheila, and Roberto, or Fr. McKnickerbocker who refers to the staff as the parish curia? Two words: authenticity and relatability.

Yes, there is a core group in every Catholic parish that lives for all the formality, pomp, and Latin references. God bless their hearts, but these are not the people in need of outreach or conversion. They've already been sold on the faith, in some cases perhaps oversold. If anything, the entire community would benefit if this *on-fire* coalition would be more concerned with how engaging they are toward others rather than how engaged everyone else is or is not.

I'm not sure if you've noticed or not, but the Catholic Church has a little public trust issue. There are a lot of contributing reasons for this so I don't want to overstate the point, but among them is the rooted reality that the Church has woven a sacristan's vocabulary into its culture. We don't use napkins; we use purificators. We don't forgive sins; we offer the sacrament of reconciliation. We don't love our neighbors; we evangelize the community. We don't feed the hungry; we practice missionary discipleship. Yes, of course we forgive sins, love our neighbors, and feed the hungry, but we're so busy sewing lace onto our language that the authenticity of our message is lost. People in the community hear our words but have no idea what any of it means.

Helpful hint for people in the religion business: "perplexing" is not an effective connection strategy.

There is often an inverse relationship between the size of our words and the depth of our meaning. "Take and eat," Jesus said. "This is my body." Very simple words with profoundly deep meaning. Compare that with, "The mission of St. Ignatius Catholic Parish is to practice reverence for Holy Eucharist and send forth disciples as soldiers for Christ." Never mind. There is no comparison.

For many, conversations using church words feel like running in shoes that are two sizes too big. It's awkward. They become self-conscious, afraid of tripping. Increasingly, they'd rather let you run on ahead without them.

LESSON 2

Be authentic and relatable, using words people understand.

STUFF TO PONDER AND DISCUSS

- Using words an average third grader would understand, answer the question: What's the best part of being Catholic?
- What part of being Catholic do you most often fake—when do you simply go through the motions or pretend to understand?
- What does the term "missionary disciple" mean to you? How would someone at the grocery store know you're a missionary disciple?

Be aware of how your words make others feel.

Zacchaeus had everything and nothing. As a chief tax collector in Jericho, all his camels had two humps. "Why would I settle for one hump when I can afford two," he boasted to the camel dealer. He lined his pockets with gold and flossed his teeth with silk. But he had no friends, at least no real friends. No one wanted the little pip-squeak around. He was, after all, a tax collector.

From there, we all know the story. News filtered through the streets that Jesus would be passing through town, and Zacchaeus, like everyone, jumped on Facebook to watch the live stream. Of course not. He put on his best tunic and went downtown to get in on the action. But being one of the least popular guys in town, he was pushed to the margins. Like the woman at the well, he was an outsider in his own community. So he climbed a tree to get a view.

As the story goes, Jesus sees him, reads the situation, and says, "Zacchaeus, scurry on down here. I want to have dinner with you."

Just pause and contemplate that scene.

Imagine how those words, spoken so publicly, felt to Zacchaeus. In his left brain, he did a quick inventory of figs, olives, bread, and wine. Would he need to send someone to the market quickly? But in his right brain, WOW! BOOM! Someone—no, not just someone, JESUS—wanted to have dinner with him! It was a transformative, life-changing moment for Zacchaeus.

Kind of hits home for us in the church industry, doesn't it? Who are the outcasts in our communities, the people hovering on the margins, who would WOW! BOOM! if offered a personal invitation from us?

The right words spoken with the right tone have that effect on people. On one level, words have a functional and informative purpose. They denote things such as, "Let's have dinner." But on an elevated and expanded plane, words convey and trigger human emotions. They have a subtext that connotes things such as, "Let's have dinner—I respect and value you and would very much like to break bread with you."

Ultimately, the language we use affects people in two ways:

1. What our words actually mean.
2. How our words make people feel.

Of critical importance here is that these are not equal. Not by any means. Whether spoken or written, how our words make people feel colors and determines what they believe our words mean. That's right. People assign meaning to our words based on the emotions triggered when they hear them. As listeners we know this, but as speakers we forget it.

Those feelings of intrigue, compassion, fear, kindness, offense, confusion, joy, empathy, warmth, ambivalence, calm, gratitude, hurt, inclusion, judgment, sadness, respect, criticism, trust, peace, support, shame, envy, anxiety, grief, friendship, amusement, support, unconditional love, and positive regard will always be a filter through which the actual meaning of our words is interpreted.

So choose words that speak with the WOW! BOOM! heart of

Christ, the heart of compassion, the heart of mercy, and the heart of inclusion. Speak with the heart of awestruck joy and gratitude for the opportunity to connect with the image of God standing before you in the moment.

LESSON 3

Be aware of how your words make others feel.

STUFF TO PONDER AND DISCUSS

- Recall a time when someone's words left you feeling positive about yourself. Recall a time when someone's words left you feeling negative about yourself.
- When have your words revealed something about you that you wished you could have taken back?
- How are the words you use in prayer different from the words you use in conversation with others? How are the topics of your prayer different from the topics of your conversations with others?

Listen first. Listen always.

Liz stirred cream into her coffee and waited eagerly for Gina to get her latte and sit down. She had wanted to text with the news last night, but decided to wait and share it in person. She leaned in, both elbows on the table, and tried her best to contain her explosive smile.

Gina began talking even before she sat down. "Boy, am I glad to see you! My life is a mess! I really need this time this morning. Phil has been traveling all week—his new boss is going to send him to an early grave. Seriously, I'm worried about his stress level. And then my mom called last night—they think Dad's cancer is back." She rubbed her temples, took a breath, and kept right on talking. "And our entire house has been brought to its knees by middle school love drama. Kaitlin was in hysterics all night because her boyfriend is moving. Frankly, I'm glad he's moving. I wish he'd move to Jupiter. I'm sorry. That's not nice." She sighed, took a drink, forced a smile, and sighed again. "How are you?"

Liz jumped on the opening. "I've invited you here this morning to evangelize you about the Catholic faith!"

Of course that's not what Liz said. That's not how friends who love one another respond to each other. She did have good news to share—she was being featured in her own gallery exhibit, a huge deal in the art community. But that could wait. Instead, she reached out and placed her hand over Gina's. "I'm fine. Tell me more about your dad."

Helpful hint for people in the religion business: Love starts with listening. That's so much harder than it sounds.

Love offers an empathetic ear that draws people from their own hearts into ours. It seeks meaningful connection and relationship before all else. If I've learned anything from my years ministering to the homeless, it's this: the most compassionate way you can show others they are loved and valued is to give them a safe, nonjudgmental space to share their story and open up about their vulnerabilities. I think this is what Jesus did.

Admittedly, not all highly engaged Catholics are going to agree with me on this point. As one middle-aged priest told me, "The most compassionate thing we can do for others is instruct them on how to correct their faults and failures." Perhaps so, but probably not. Perhaps that's why our pews are increasingly empty.

There is a canyon-sized difference between hearing what someone is saying and truly listening to them. When all we do is hear the other person, we are mostly concerned with the dialog in our own heads. We may be hearing them, but we are actually listening to ourselves. As they're speaking, the voice in our head is preoccupied with its own conversation: *What does this mean to me? How do I feel about what this person is saying? How should I respond?* It is as though we are regarding everything that's being shared as mere data which we run through our own personal relevancy and response filters.

When we truly listen to another person, however, we are interested in the dialog that's going on within the mind of the speaker and we seek to draw it out. We recognize that what they are saying is the tip of a proverbial iceberg, and we want to see and comprehend what's beneath it and behind it. It's an act of compassion, the point where communication becomes communion. We want to know them.

LESSON 4

Listen first. Listen always.

STUFF TO PONDER AND DISCUSS

- How do you feel when you're having a discussion with someone who may be hearing what you're saying, but only listening to what they themselves are thinking?
- What biases and prejudices do you hold that perhaps get in the way of truly listening to someone who sees the world differently than you do?
- What is the most compassionate way to respond to someone who is voicing an opinion you find objectionable?

Avoid abstractions. Be concrete.

Jesus wasn't big on abstractions. His whole jam was about making things tangible and concrete. Think about it. God is abstract; Jesus made God tangible. Forgiveness is a concept; Jesus made it concrete. We can say the same for healing, compassion, and the Kingdom of God. When a couple of the boys wanted to talk about feeding people (a concept), badda-bing! loaves and fishes (tangible). In fact, up until Jesus, the very idea of a Messiah was just that—an idea. Jesus made it real—on earth as it is in heaven.

So when the Pharisees sauntered up looking for a primetime theoretical throw-down about paying taxes, Jesus would have none of it. He was not about to get suckered into an abstraction distraction.

"Whose image is on the coin?" he asked, making it concrete. "Give to Caesar what is Caesar's and give to God what is God's." He repeated this pattern time and again throughout his ministry.

Perhaps the most important and most difficult thing the Church needs to do is follow suit. And frankly, we're really good at it.

I mean REALLY GOOD at it.

The Catholic Church is great at all the things that make Christianity concrete, such as gathering people around the table for Eucharist, feeding the hungry, sheltering the homeless, offering forgiveness, visiting the sick, and so forth.

But as good as we are at the concrete stuff that matters, we often seem equally bad at talking about it. In our dialog, we love the conceptual realm. Instead of engaging the world as Jesus did with stories about good Samaritans and lost coins, we'll talk endlessly to an increasingly empty room about contrition, confirmation, and consecration. From annulments to zucchettos, we proudly, sometimes even arrogantly, pontificate about apostolic succession, salvation, and the like.

Helpful hint for people in the religion business: arrogant pontification is a better strategy for politics than religion. And I'm not sure it's even a good strategy for politics.

To clarify, it's not as though the conceptual realm is verboten. Not at all. But know your audience. When physicists meet up at their annual physics convention, they can and probably should order up a couple pitchers of root beer and argue about a unified theory until the bubbles go to their heads. Back at home, however, when the neighbors gather for a barbecue and the guys cluster around the grills, it's best to talk about concrete things such as lawn mowers and baseball. If specifically asked about why the bat sometimes breaks, the physicist among them has permission to talk briefly about collision force, with an emphasis on briefly.

Way back in 1936 when Dale Carnegie wrote *How to Win Friends and Influence People,* his list of six ways to become likable included "Talk in terms of the other person's interest." This is what Jesus did when he talked about shepherds and vineyards. He related everything to the concrete world people lived in, were interested in, and understood.

LESSON 5

Avoid abstractions. Be concrete.

STUFF TO PONDER AND DISCUSS

- What is the difference between something that is conceptual and something that is concrete?
- In what ways is the kingdom of God an idea? In what ways is it a reality?
- What is the role of faith in connecting daily experience with spiritual truths?

Be generous with joy.

I had a spiritually abrasive realization at my local Department of Motor Vehicles. It felt as though someone had taken a Brillo pad to my heart. First, let me emphasize that, with the exception of nervous sixteen-year-olds going for their driver's test, I've never heard anyone say, "I'm really pumped that I get to go to the DMV!" Most people would rather be force-fed roofing nails.

So here was my scratchy awakening: I saw more people smile at the DMV than at church.

Yup. Gulp.

On the scale ranging from root canal to beach vacation, where do you think "church" falls for most people? Judging from a scan of the faces at most Catholic Masses I've attended, I'd reckon "church" falls only one notch north of "tax audit" on the joy meter. And that's reading the faces of the people who are actually in church!

As you greet these same people on their way into or out of Mass, they smile broadly, laugh generously, and seem like the happiest people on earth—as long as you're talking about the weather, the Packers, their children, or anything else that isn't religion. As soon as you bring up the gospel or Eucharist or the kingdom of God, faces turn somber and serious, like you're discussing cancer test results.

What happens?

As Christians, we basically invented joy and alleluia! Well, maybe that's an overstatement. We didn't invent it, but we made a religion out of it. We're Empty Tomb people, Easter people, who turned funerals from black to white, from darkness to light. Yet the same people who happily belt out *"Buy me some peanuts and crackerjack"* at baseball games won't move their lips for an Alleluia acclamation at Mass.

Before we accuse folks of checking their joy at the door, we need to be uncomfortably honest about church culture. Perhaps people don't express joy at Mass because they've been conditioned to believe stone-faced stoicism is the more culturally acceptable expression. After all, it's RELIGION. This is serious wrath-of-God business.

Sure, there's a conceptual promise of eternal reward, but it's paired with the very concrete notion of eternal fire and damnation. The implied message most of us have received since we were knee high is clear: This is no laughing matter! We don't go to Mass to celebrate and party like wayward college students on spring break; we go to be contrite out of obligation. So sit there quietly.

A 2018 survey conducted by The Karma Group revealed a remarkable joy gap in the Catholic Church. (Author disclaimer: I serve as principal and Chief Strategy officer at The Karma Group). Among survey participants, nearly sixty percent of non-religious people and inactive Catholics identified humor as one of their top five values in life, but only thirty-eight percent of active Catholics agree.

Grab the arms of your chair and grip that thought. Six out of ten people who do not engage religion—including those who were raised Catholic but are inactive—list humor as one of the top five values in life. Fewer than four out of ten churchgoing Catholics feel the same way.

Here's the real kicker: less than one percent of all survey participants listed humor as a value prioritized by the Catholic Church, and that was thematically consistent across active Catholics, inactive Catholics, non-Catholics, and non-religious.

You don't need a slide rule to calculate the disconnect here. Granted, there is a technical difference between humor and joy, but with margins this wide let's not kid ourselves. Perhaps it'll help if I frame it up for you again with a handy graphic:

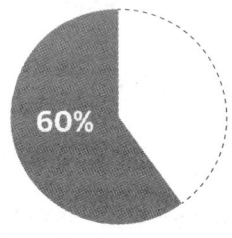 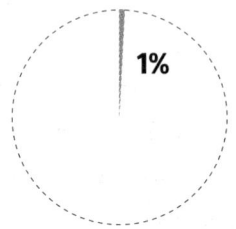

People who list HUMOR as a Top 5 value **in their life**

People who list HUMOR as a Top 5 value **of Cath Church**

You see the problem, right?

Maybe, and I'm just spit-balling here, we could better relate to people if we'd be a little more joyful?

LESSON 6

Be generous with joy.

STUFF TO PONDER AND DISCUSS

- In what ways are humor and joy the same? In what ways are they different?
- When does prayer make you smile? When does prayer ever make you laugh?
- What holds us back from relaxing and simply being ourselves among friends when we're in church?

Meet people where they're at and simply walk alongside them.

When I was barely five years old, my mother enrolled me in summer swimming lessons at the local high school. I needed to learn how to swim, she told me, so I wouldn't drown.

Stick with that logic for a moment.

In my five-year-old mind, it led to only one conclusion: I would drown if I got in the water. Hence, I should stay out of the water.

Up until the first day of lessons, I had never been in a pool you didn't inflate with air from your own lungs. I had never been in water that was more than mid-shin deep; nor had I been inside a locker room or smelled chlorine. The whole scene was overwhelming.

Standing on the pool deck, I heard the swim teacher call out instructions to get into the water. I froze. I didn't want to die, which is clearly what would happen since I didn't know how to swim.

"Just jump in!" she encouraged like a smiling TV evangelist selling religion as if it's a street drug. That was NOT going to happen. She tried again but got the same result. And again. And again.

Finally, another teacher named Dave came over, picked me up, and said, "This is for your own good, you lily-livered little chicken," and threw me into the deep end of the pool.

No! Of course that didn't happen. That would have been terribly cruel and abusive.

Dave took my hand and sat on the edge of the pool with me, our legs dangling in the water. He encouraged me to splash. Eventually, he showed me how to ease myself into the water without letting go of the edge; how to put my face in the water and blow bubbles; how to pick up one foot, then the other, and then both feet.

The first teacher wanted me to meet her where she was at—having fun in the water. The more she encouraged, the more I resisted. Dave met me where I was at—alone, frightened, standing on the pool deck. He walked with me at my pace, not pushing me until I was ready for the next step.

This seems to be Jesus' approach. When meeting disciples on the road to Emmaus, for example, he didn't get in their faces with, "Hey! It's me! So chin up!" Instead, he simply met them where they were at—forlorn, grieving, and confused—and walked with them, slowly drawing them out until they were able to see for themselves. It's the prodigal son approach.

Perhaps the most critical thing about communicating and connecting with people is found in what we don't say. It is entirely ineffective to stand in the pool and try to coax people to jump in. Whether they want to or not is irrelevant at that point. It's just overwhelming. Likewise, trying to shake them with judgmental words, telling them what's wrong with them, is flat out cruel. We shouldn't try to bully people into Jesus. Yikes!

Instead, it is far more effective to sit alongside people on the edge of the pool or the side of the fire, to meet them where they're at—wherever they're at, and simply companion them as they journey forward at their own pace. They will get there eventually, as long as we support them, love them, and listen to them.

LESSON 7

Meet people where they're at and simply walk alongside them.

STUFF TO PONDER AND DISCUSS

- How does it feel to have someone coax or coerce you into something you aren't ready or motivated to do, even if it's good for you such as jogging or eating kale? How do you respond?
- How is an invitation different from encouragement? How is encouragement different from coercion?
- In a person's spiritual journey, how important is the opportunity for self-discovery?

Give yourself a short sabbath between thoughts and words.

They brought the woman to him. Caught her red-handed like a kid with her hand in the cookie jar, except worse. So much worse.

They caught her in the very act of being human!

Granted, we're all human. We all have faults and failings, but this was the dark side of being human—adultery. It's not like they caught her in the act of sneaking an extra brownie—also a very human thing to do. This was big, a direct violation of Number Six on the Top Ten list of ways to bring down God's wrath. She was putting the whole community at risk. A price would have to be paid.

So what would this love-mercy-and-forgiveness preacher say? That it's OK? That people can break the rules willy-nilly without consequence? That their ancestors had lugged the Ark of the Covenant around the desert for no good reason—it all doesn't matter anyway?

Or would he admit that all this pie-eyed idealism crumbles when confronted with reality? Would he respect how the law had stood the test of time, how it must always stand, and this woman should be stoned in accordance with that law?

Jesus looked into the terrified brown eyes of the woman. Then he looked at the set jawlines of the accusers.

Ugh. There was so much wrong here.

Where to begin? It felt like he was the one on trial, at least more so than the woman. Was love on trial? Was the whole idea of forgiveness on trial?

Taking a deep breath, Jesus unleashed a moralistic firehouse, dousing them in the theology of the body, reverence for all life, the sacredness of tradition, the promise of redemption, sanctification by grace, and the spiritual problem of having sinister motivations. He dizzied them with his depth, dazzled them with his command of the teachings, and disoriented them with all the contradictions inherent in the human condition.

Actually, he did none of that. He drew in the dirt.

Helpful hint for people in the religion business: dizzying, dazzling, and disorienting are not effective ways to inspire curiosity and foster understanding.

After speaking the famous words about only throwing stones if you're without sin, Jesus gave everyone space to process and self-reflect. That would be enough for one day. Religion, like a fine wine or a rich dessert, is often best savored in contemplative sips and appreciative bites. You need time to fully digest it if you're going to incorporate it into your life. When we feed people religion faster than they can absorb it, they either become intoxicated on it (fundamentalist), or sick of it (agnostic/atheist), or first intoxicated and then sick.

There is something to be said for taking a few minutes to draw in the dirt. It's like giving ourselves a short sabbath between thoughts and words, rest time to center our minds and slow our heartbeats. The spirit needs space to breathe. Light needs a crack through which to enter.

When talking about faith with others, it might be most effective and perhaps most compassionate to pace yourself. The pilgrimage to deep spirituality is a journey that unfolds over a lifetime, so there is no need to squeeze it all into a single conversation. Give yourself and others time to ponder the mystery of it all.

LESSON 8

Give yourself a short sabbath between thoughts and words.

STUFF TO PONDER AND DISCUSS

- When pondering your own faith, do you have more questions or answers? How do you share your questions with others?
- When does silence speak more effectively than words? Have you ever experienced this?
- Once you've scattered a few seeds, what makes it difficult to trust God to provide the sun and the rain?

We live in a Buzzfeed world. Headlines that promise a list of things are known in the communications industry as click bait. We can't resist them. I must review *The 5 Hottest Minivans of the Year*, even if I have no interest in minivans, which I don't—let's be clear about that. It's the same with *15 Celebrities Who've Gotten Better with Age*, *8 Super Foods That Will Reduce Cancer Risk*, and *The 10 Gadgets That Will Make Cooking Easier*.

The magic formula isn't simply in the fact that it's a numbered list. It's a numbered list that promises a simple way to discover something new or make life easier. Imagine if the Catholic Church had used this formula all along:

- 10 Commandments That Will Make You Happy Forever
- 8 Beatitudes That Are Guaranteed to Improve Your Sleep
- 7 Gifts of the Holy Spirit That Will Give Your Life Deeper Meaning
- 7 Sacraments That Will Rock Your Life

In that spirit, let's conclude with a Buzzfeed summary that distills all this down to a simple list.

8 Easy Ways to Communicate That Are Guaranteed to Connect with Others

1. Be like God and keep it simple.

2. Be authentic and relatable, using words people understand.

3. Be aware of how your words make others feel.

4. Listen first. Listen always.

5. Avoid abstractions. Be concrete.

6. Be generous with joy.

7. Meet people where they're at and simply walk alongside them.

8. Give yourself a short sabbath between thoughts and words.